BAT,
BALL,
GLOVE

BAT, BALL, GLOVE

The Making of Major League
Baseball Gear

◆

William Jaspersohn

LITTLE, BROWN AND COMPANY

Boston ◆ Toronto ◆ London

Books by WILLIAM JASPERSOHN

The Ballpark: One Day Behind the Scenes at a Major League Game
A Day in the Life of a Marine Biologist
A Day in the Life of a Television News Reporter
A Day in the Life of a Veterinarian
Grounded, a novel
How Life on Earth Began
How People First Lived
How the Forest Grew
How the Universe Began
Ice Cream
Magazine: Behind the Scenes at Sports Illustrated
Motorcycle: The Making of a Harley-Davidson

For Victor and Sarah Swenson

First edition

Library of Congress Cataloging-in-Publication Data

Jaspersohn, William.
Bat, ball, glove.

Summary: Describes how and where baseball equipment is made.
1. Baseball — Equipment and supplies — Juvenile
literature. [1. Baseball — Equipment and supplies]
I. Title.
GV879.7.J37   1989   796.357'028   88-27198
ISBN 0-316-45820-1

10   9   8   7   6   5   4   3   2   1
MPC
Published simultaneously in Canada
by Little, Brown & Company (Canada) Limited

PRINTED IN THE UNITED STATES OF AMERICA

Glove

When Ozzie Smith needs a new baseball glove, he does not go to a sporting goods store to buy one. Instead, the star shortstop for the St. Louis Cardinals does what hundreds of other major league players routinely do — he calls Bill Smith,

the manager for professional sales at the Rawlings Sporting Goods Company in nearby Fenton, Missouri, and says, "Bill, I need a new glove. Could you maybe fix me up with something pretty soon?"

It is two-thirty on a humid afternoon in early June, and Bill Smith sits in his air-conditioned office in the chrome-and-glass Rawlings building, taking notes for Ozzie's order. In an album in his home in St. Louis, Bill has a photo of himself with Ozzie Smith, the two of them smiling at the camera like the professional comrades that they are. Over the years, Bill Smith has gotten Ozzie dozens of fine baseball gloves.

"What happened, Oz? Somebody steal your gamer?"

"No, but it's starting to go soft, and I'm going to have to start using my practice glove for games pretty soon. I figure if I got a new glove for practice, I could start breaking it in, and have it ready for the last sixty games of the season."

"Well, you're in luck," says Bill Smith. He has several of the model Ozzie uses, the Pro 12TC, in his office. "I can bring them down to the stadium in an hour."

"Hey, that'd be great," says Ozzie Smith.

Bill Smith works with Ted Sizemore, Rawlings' vice president of baseball development, supplying equipment to players and teams throughout the major leagues. Teams order baseballs, uniforms, bats, balls, catcher's equipment, and helmets from Rawlings. Players who have signed equipment contracts with Rawlings order gloves. It's a happy arrangement, for in return for using Rawlings gloves exclusively, a player gets to choose and keep as many gloves as his contract calls for from the sixty-four different pro models that Rawlings manufactures. And if a player needs a new glove right away, Bill Smith can send him one — from his office or from the company warehouse in Springfield, Missouri — in less than twenty-four hours.

Ted Sizemore speaks glowingly of Rawlings gloves, and not just because he works for the company. In 1969, as a second baseman for the Los Angeles Dodgers, Ted won Rookie of the Year honors using a Rawlings Pro 5X-TC, and, throughout his career — with the Dodgers, Cardinals, Phillies, Red Sox, and Cubs — he never used any other model. "I was always a good fielder," he says, "in Little League, high school, the minors, the majors. But my glove made me a better one. It's a privilege to work for this company."

The glove that Bill Smith will bring to Ozzie Smith was manufactured here, at the Rawlings factory in Ava, Missouri.

The man who designed Ozzie's glove — and who designs every baseball glove in the line — is Rawlings' master glove designer, Bob Clevenhagen. Only the third glove designer in the company's hundred-year history, Bob both creates new glove models and modifies older ones to improve them. For a new glove, he starts by sketching patterns of its different parts on cardboard then cutting the parts out and laying them together to see how they fit.

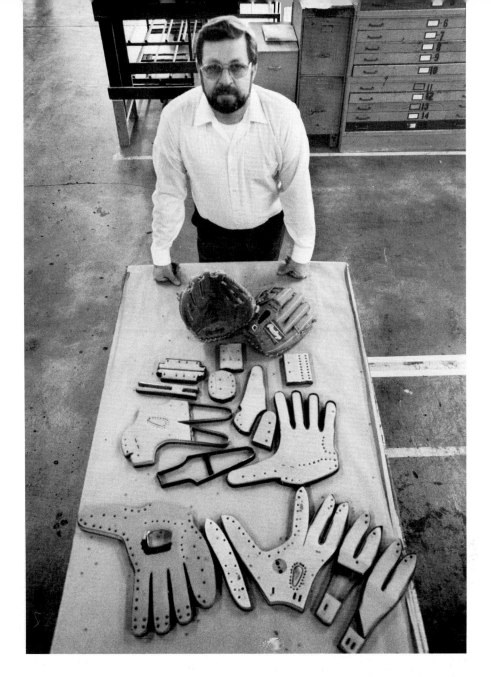

Once a glove design has been approved for production by the home office in Fenton, Bob orders cutting dies of the glove's different parts from a Rawlings machine shop in Licking, Missouri. The cutting dies, modeled from the shapes of the cardboard patterns, look a lot like heavy-duty cookie cutters, and in a way, that's how they work. On average, there are fifteen leather parts in a glove, not including lacing, and the sharp-edged, heavy steel dies ensure that those parts are cut to precise tolerances.

When the time comes to make new baseball gloves, a worker rolls out a batch of the cowhides stored in the company's warehouse and sorts and groups them according to color. The hides, which come from a company-owned tannery in Tullahoma, Tennessee, are beautiful things, the leather strong, soft, and supple. The worker looks for imperfections in the leather — nicks, holes, and scratches — tagging the best for use in making major-league model gloves.

Parts of a Glove and Where on the Cowhide They Come From

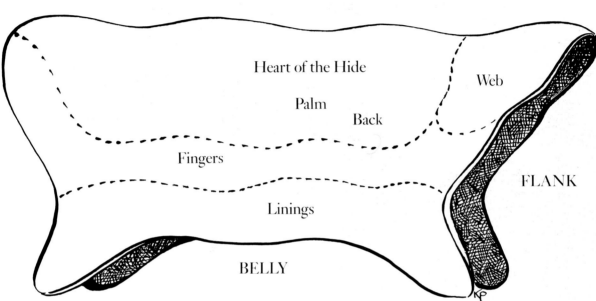

BUTT

NECK

Heart of the Hide

Web

Palm

Back

Fingers

FLANK

Linings

BELLY

On average, a cowhide measures twenty-six square feet, and if it's cut properly, the company can expect to make three or four gloves from it. Different areas of the hide are used for different glove parts, with the strongest, most supple area, known as the heart, used for that part of the glove that will take the most abuse, the pocket.

In the cutting room, the leather is laid out on a hard maple bench, and a worker positions the die over the hide. Of all the steps required to make a glove, this is the most exacting. The die must be positioned precisely over the correct area of hide — belly for linings, flank for fingers, neck for webbing, heart for palm and back — and the worker must consider the grain, or arrangement of the leather fibers (which determine the leather's texture), and orient the die accordingly. To manage all that and still cut as many pieces from the hide as possible would seem to require a lot of time. And yet, a skilled worker can usually position a die in a matter of seconds.

Once the die is positioned, the worker swings a hood-shaped steel stamping machine over it. The stamper is capable of exerting four thousand pounds of downward pressure. When the worker depresses a thumb button, the machine crunches down on the die, which, in turn, stamps out the glove part.

The leather pieces destined to become the palms for a new batch of gloves go to a worker who, using a simple printing machine, stamps them with the Rawlings name, or logo, as it's called, along with the glove's model name and other related information.

These and other parts are then color sorted so that, later on, each glove can be constructed of parts of the same color.

The next big step in making a baseball glove is the sewing that must be done. Each operator is responsible for only one part of the sewing operation; so, for example, while one operator sews the Rawlings *R* on what will become the back of the glove, another sews together the two pieces where the hand and fingers will go, called the lining. In addition, strips of fuzzy, dark blue felt, for padding, are sewn onto the lining's first three fingers.

Meanwhile, a third operator sews strips of gray leather, called welting, along what will be the back and outer edges of the glove's fingers. Welting tends not to stretch and thus adds stability to the fingers so that the finished glove holds its shape better. "The only gloves that don't include welting," says Bob Clevenhagen, "are catcher's mitts, since they don't have the same kind of finger configurations as other gloves."

Once the welting operation is done, a red "Rawlings" label gets stitched to the glove's back piece.

The part of a baseball glove between the thumb and first finger is known as the web, and, depending on the positions they play and what feels comfortable to them, major league players like gloves with different kinds of web configurations. Outfielders, for instance, tend to like an open, H-shaped web, because they can sight oncoming fly balls through it and the web's flexibility helps them snare balls they must stretch for. Infielders, by contrast, usually prefer a solid, "closed" web, because it's stiffer, and thus the ball tends not to get stuck in it as easily. To meet players' requirements, Rawlings offers ten different web designs, some of which require hand weaving, and all of which require special sewing.

The last big sewing step before all the glove parts are assembled is called "closing the shell." In this step, the two pieces of leather that make up the outside, or shell, of the glove, are sewn together. The problem is, these pieces have to be sewn together inside out. How do the glove makers turn the shell and each of its fingers so that the leather's smooth side faces out the way it's supposed to?

Simple. The company has fashioned a device with two thin steel rods facing tip to tip. A worker slips a finger of the shell over the upper rod and steps on a pedal, which causes the two rod tips to push together, clamping the finger at its tip. Now it's an easy matter for the worker to pull down on the shell and turn the finger right-side out. He does this for each of the fingers (it takes several seconds per finger), and the finished shell is ready to be "laid off" — stretched and shaped and smoothed on aluminum "hot hands" electrically heated to three hundred degrees Fahrenheit.

The three major parts of the glove — shell, web, and lining — are now ready for assembly. The lining is slipped over another aluminum hand form, and a worker tugs the finished shell over the lining until the two fit snugly together.

Then, using a small, noisy but powerful machine, the worker punches holes along the heel of both the shell and the lining and reinforces each hole with a flat, stainless-steel ring called a grommet. The grommet-reinforced holes allow the shell and lining to be easily laced together later with rawhide lacing.

Bob Clevenhagen says major league baseball players generally prefer gloves with firm, dense padding that won't fall apart easily and will help the glove hold its shape — and thus, its catching power — even when catching screaming liners. To meet that preference, Rawlings uses half inch thicknesses of the firmest, densest wool felt it can find to pad the thumbs, little fingers, and heels of its pro-model gloves.

After that, each glove gets a squirt of sticky synthetic grease in the palm area between the shell and the lining. The grease keeps the leather supple, helps the shell and lining stick together, and also makes it easier, later on, to form a good, deep pocket in the glove.

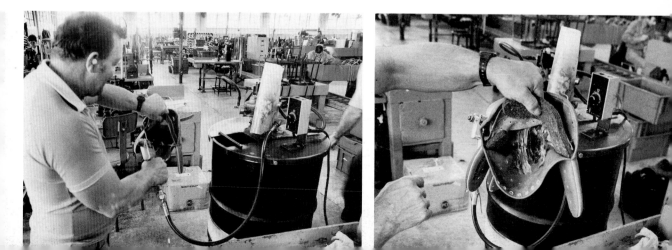

Lacing is the last major step in a glove's construction. Each person in the lacing department is responsible for only one part of the total operation, and there are five lacing steps altogether. First, the pads that will support the player's thumb and little finger are laced to the lining and shell; second, the shell and lining are laced together along the bottom of the pocket; third, the webbing is laced into place between the thumb and first finger; fourth, lacing is run between the glove's fingertips and wrapped along the top edge of the web; and fifth, the shell and lining are laced together along their grommeted heels. In all, it takes eight to ten feet of rawhide and a solid hour of work to lace each glove properly.

Even though the gloves are carefully constructed, each must be inspected for flaws. If a glove is nicked or scratched, if the colors of the leather parts don't match, if a finger is wrinkled or any part mis-stitched, it is rejected as a major league glove. As long as it's properly constructed, Rawlings will probably still sell the glove, but a major league player — who depends on the glove and wants the best — will never use it. "Only perfect gloves," says Bob Clevenhagen, "or as near as perfect as we can make them, go to our major-leaguers."

Now the finished pro-model gloves go for their final lay-off. Each glove is gently hammered down onto a glove-shaped aluminum form to open the finger stalls, the places where the player's fingers go. A specially trained worker shapes the pocket by pounding it with a gourd-shaped maple mallet. Excess threads are snipped off with an embroidery knife. The glove is scrutinized, tried on, the pocket pounded.

Only when the worker is satisfied that the finished glove looks and feels right is it boxed. Gloves for Ozzie Smith, Dale Murphy, Tony Gwinn, Robin Yount, Wally Joyner, Mark McGwire, Lance Parrish, Cal Ripken, Jr., Ryne Sandberg, Dave Winfield, and hundreds of other major league players are so boxed. The glove that Bill Smith will give Ozzie Smith this afternoon was boxed and sent to Bill one month ago. Bill's been keeping it safe for Ozzie in his bottom-left-hand desk drawer.

Ball

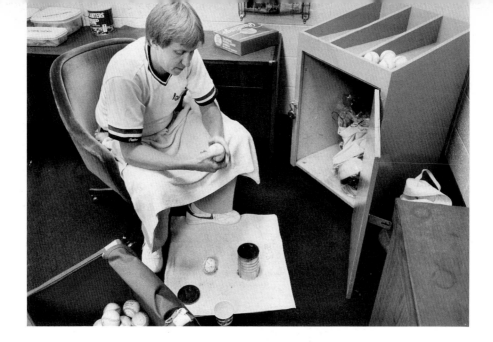

In the umpires' room in Busch Stadium, on the same afternoon that Bill Smith will rendezvous with Ozzie Smith, Frank Copenbarger, the assistant equipment manager for the St. Louis Cardinals, rubs mud on twelve dozen baseballs destined to be used in a game later that night against the New York Mets. A club towel covers Frank's lap. Another is spread on the floor. Frank dips the first three fingers of his right hand into a can of the silty mud, swirls the mud across his other fingers, picks up a new, shiny white baseball, and rotates the ball swiftly in his hands. The wet mud stains the pristine ball a uniform, pale creamy brown. It also raises the grain of the ball's leather, making the ball easier to grip and to throw. As sacrilegious as discoloring 144 baseballs per game may seem, every home team in the major leagues has been doing it for decades. The mud, which comes from a river somewhere near the Delaware, is called Lena Blackburne's Baseball Rubbing Mud, and it's sold to teams by the family of the late Lena Blackburne, a onetime pitching coach for the Chicago White Sox. Out of fear that others will encroach on their business, the family won't reveal the source of their mud. They only say that it is harvested at night, in rowboats, that it is carefully sifted before it is canned, and that a single can fetches seventy-five dollars.

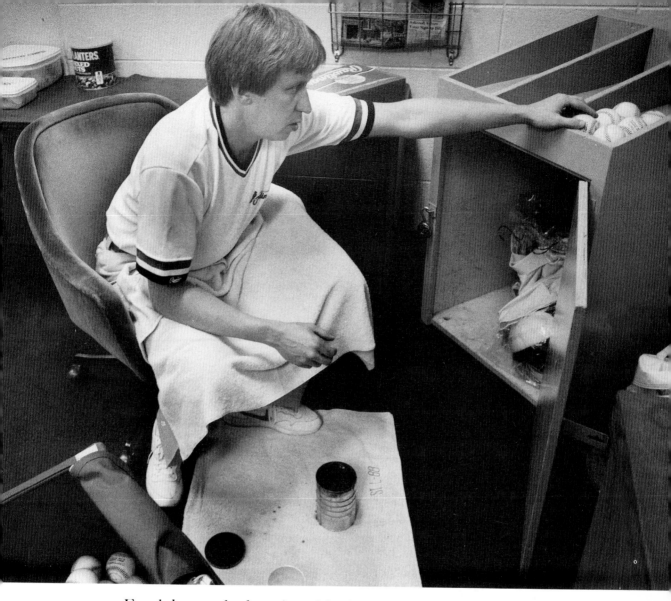

Frank leaves the last six rubbed-up baseballs on a stand for the home-plate umpire. These will be the first six balls used in tonight's game, and they'll probably be used up — fouled off, hit for a home run, or scuffed during play and thrown out by the umpires — before the game is two outs old. Little wonder, then, that the Cardinals and other pro teams buy baseballs for themselves at a rate of about fifteen hundred dozen a season.

Rawlings, the official supplier of baseballs to the major leagues, manufactures its baseballs in Haiti. So secret are some of the manufacturing processes, however, that Rawlings does not allow visitors into any of its ball-making plants. Officials at Rawlings in Missouri will only describe *generally* how they make baseballs. To begin with, they say, if you cut a baseball open, you would find that it's composed of a number of different layers. The center of the ball, called the pill, is actually a small sphere of rubber-covered, cushioned cork. Around its cement-covered surface, top-secret winding machines wind three layers of wool and one layer of cotton yarn. When the last layer of yarn is wound to the desired thickness, a film of glue is applied to keep the yarn from unwinding, and thin but durable white cowhide covers are sewn over the outer surface.

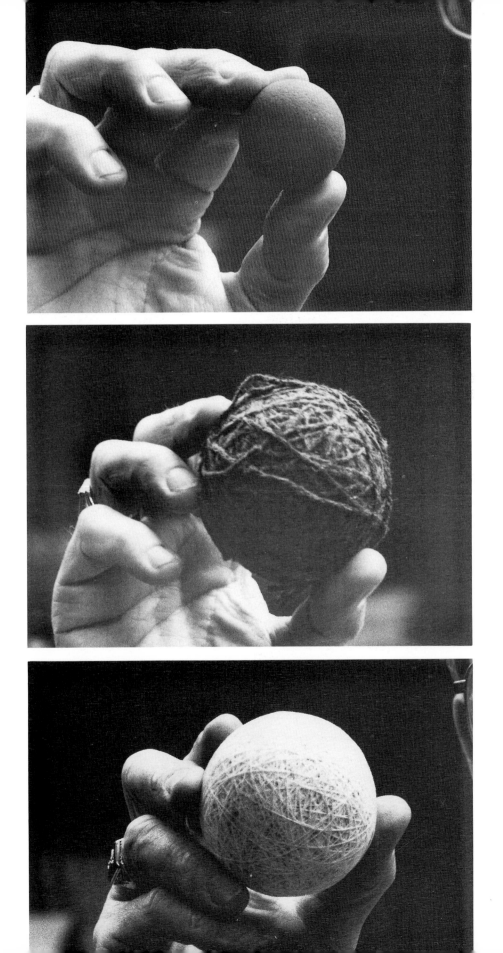

The two figure-eight-shaped covers are sewn over the ball by hand. But first, a stapler staples them to the ball to hold them in place as the stitches are applied.

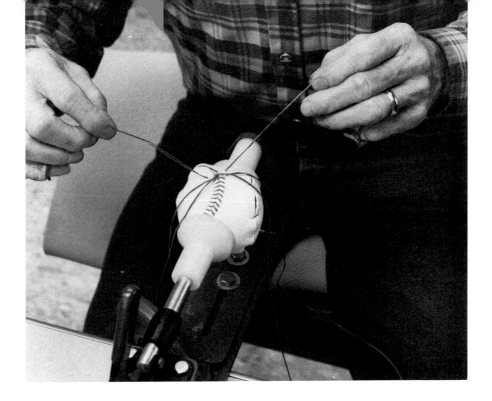

Once the covers are positioned and their prepunched holes properly aligned, the stitcher can begin the actual stitching. Two needles are used to draw two, forty-four-inch lengths of waxed red cotton thread through the holes, and the stitcher must be careful not to skip any hole and to draw the thread flat and tight. The job isn't easy. Getting the needles through the holes takes a lot of poking and tugging, and the stitcher's arms get tired yanking the thread. In all, there are 108 stitches on a baseball, and, on average, it takes a stitcher ten minutes to complete them all.

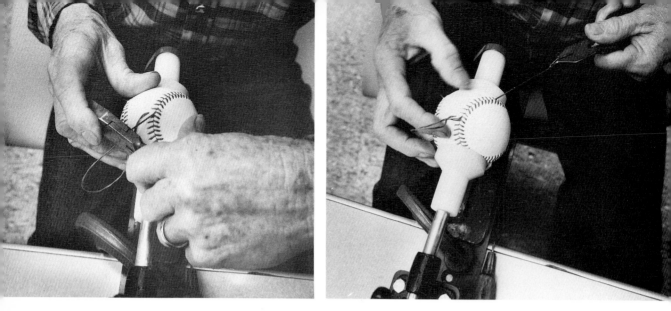

The 108th stitch poses two problems for the stitcher: namely, how do you cut the thread without leaving a piece of it dangling from the baseball, and how do you prevent the thread from working loose and all the stitching from coming unraveled?

The answer lies in "hiding" the last stitch, and here's how it's done. As soon as the stitcher pulls the thread through the last hole on the cover, he pushes the needle under the long seam until the point comes out about ten stitches down from the last. He pulls the needle free, thereby locking the last stitch under the ten others. The stitcher can now snip the thread, knowing the stitches won't come unraveled, and he can hide the protruding end of the cut thread under the seam with the aid of a fine-pointed awl.

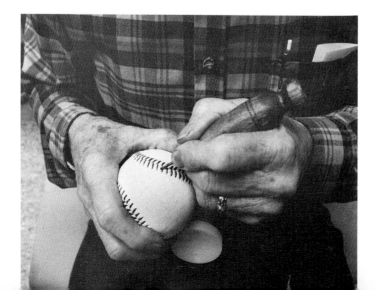

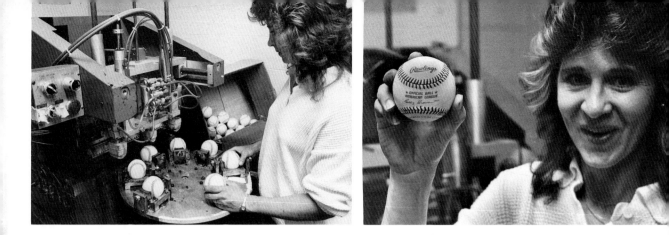

Once their seams are machine-rolled under light pressure for fifteen seconds to compress the stitches and produce a consistent surface, baseballs manufactured in Rawlings' Haiti plant are shipped by air to the Ava plant for stamping. If a ball is destined for the National League, it is stamped in black ink. The stamping reads

Rawlings

★OFFICIAL BALL★

NATIONAL LEAGUE

William D. White, PRES.

CUSHIONED CORK CENTER

RO-N

If a ball is destined for the American League, it is stamped in light blue ink. And its stamping reads

Rawlings

★OFFICIAL BALL★

AMERICAN LEAGUE

Bobby Brown, PRES.

CUSHIONED CORK CENTER

RO-A

"RO" is Rawlings' code for its major-league model ball. "N" stands for National, "A" for American.

Once the balls are stamped, they're ready for inspection. The inspectors sit in a temperature-controlled room and, like nimble egg candlers, make split-second judgments. If a ball shows the slightest tick, dot, nick, speck, mark, or discoloration, it is rejected. If it has a loose stitch, it is rejected. If it doesn't look round or if the stitches are raised, it is rejected. If it doesn't measure between 9 and 9¼ inches, it is rejected.

Finally, if a ball's weight doesn't register between 5 and 5¼ ounces on an electronic scale, it is rejected. These weights and circumferences are major league specifications, and one of the satisfactions about the game of baseball is that these specifications have endured since 1872. True, materials and construction methods have changed somewhat. The rubber-cushioned cork center didn't replace rubberless cork centers until 1926. Horsehide was the official cover material for generations until baseball commissioner Bowie Kuhn authorized the use of cowhide in 1974. Better yarn-winding processes now ensure baseballs without any lumps or dead spots. Still, a baseball hit today by Darryl Strawberry is exactly the same size and weight and is made of exactly the same combination of materials as a baseball hit by Babe Ruth over a half century ago. "It has to be the same," a Rawlings official says, "otherwise how could you measure players' performances from year to year? You couldn't. There has to be consistency."

Given these concerns, the people in the inspection room at Ava routinely reject two baseballs for every one they release for sale to the major leagues. The chosen balls are individually hand wrapped in squares of white tissue and cartoned like eggs in groups of a dozen. The cosmetically less-perfect balls, designated "commercial stock," are also wrapped and boxed, but these suffer a fate common to any serviceable but less-than-perfect player: they are sent to the lower leagues.

Uniform

On the top step of the home-team dugout in Busch Stadium, the star infielder/outfielder for the St. Louis Cardinals, Jose Oquendo, sits waiting for the start of infield practice. He wears the team uniform: red cap, red stockings, snowy white double-knit polyester pants and pullover jersey, the latter emblazoned with the colorful team logo. It's hard to decide which part of the logo is more beautiful: the two red cardinals perched on the glowing gold bat, the bat itself, or the succinct cursive letters spelling the team name. Jose Oquendo says he likes the entire uniform, it fits him to a T, and if he happens to soil it unduly before the game, he takes comfort knowing there is another just like it on a wooden hanger, back in his locker in the clubhouse.

CIRCA 1904   CIRCA 1915   CIRCA 1930

    Baseball uniforms have not always looked so handsome or so modern. In 1851 (some sources say 1849), the New York Knickerbocker Baseball Club introduced the first baseball uniforms, consisting of full-length navy blue trousers, webbed belts, white shirts, and straw hats. A few years later, they and other teams were wearing short-billed, cricket-style caps. In 1868, the Cincinnati Red Stockings took to the field in knee-length knickerbocker pants. Opposing players hooted when they saw these breeches. "Sissy pants!" they shouted. Nonetheless, within a few years, knee-length pants became the norm for all baseball teams, and by the 1880s, uniforms included long-sleeved woolen shirts (some with lace fronts, all with big "sun" collars), woolen knickers, knee-length colored stockings, and billed caps. Lace fronts went out of fashion around the turn of the century, and half sleeves replaced full-length sleeves on baseball shirts. But not until the early 1900s did the floppy sun collar disappear and the baseball shirt begin to resemble somewhat the shirts worn by major-leaguers today. Trim appeared — around the collar, down the front of the shirt, and around the sleeve ends — making the shirts more colorful. Zipper-front shirts, introduced in the 1930s, were as popular as button-front models until the beginning of the 1950s. For a short while in the early fifties, innovative minor league teams tried wearing knit shirts and shorts as uniforms. This innovation fizzled. Scratchy, loose-fitting wool uniforms finally evolved to more tailored styles in the early 1960s. Designers at Rawlings, which had been making baseball uniforms since the company's first year of business in 1887, and designers at other sporting goods companies, began tapering shirts at the waist, pants at the hips, thighs, and knees. Instead of blousing pants at the knee, players began blousing them at the calf. Some teams requested that players' names be sewn across the backs of their shirts, making their identification by fans easier. Numbers, letters, and trim colors became brighter. Logos became bigger and flashier. Uniforms became so colorful and formfitting that, by the 1970s, players looked like streamlined peacocks. Uniforms once labeled "100% wool" were now labeled "100% polyester." Players liked the new material because it stretched but retained its shape. Equipment managers loved it because it was durable and easy to clean. They bought washing machines for their clubhouses. Dry-cleaning accounts were erased from club ledgers. Three or four washing machines could do in half an hour with polyester what had taken a dry cleaner half a day to do with wool. Uniform material became so lightweight and formfitting that players took to wearing thigh-length cotton-knit undershorts so that no telltale underwear line would show. Vanity and practicality had attained equilibrium.

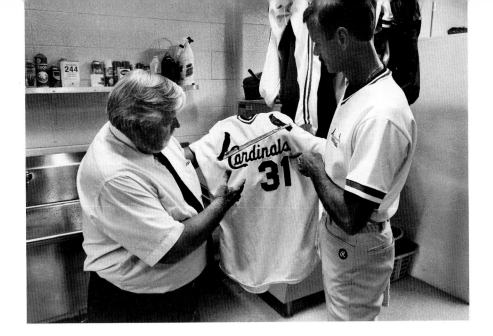

Today, twenty-three of the twenty-six major league teams wear uniforms made by Rawlings, and they place most of their orders in December, during a gathering of owners from all the clubs, known as the winter meetings. In February, Bill Smith and three Rawlings staff crews armed with sizing charts, measuring tapes, and sample uniforms, fly to the spring-training camps in Florida, Arizona, and California. There they measure new players for uniforms and check to make sure that veterans haven't fattened or thinned over the winter. The measurements for each player are sent to the Rawlings uniform-manufacturing plant in Licking, Missouri, which has the daunting task of making and delivering five thousand uniforms and pregame shirts before the opening day of the baseball season in early April. Thereafter, Bill Smith and several others on the Rawlings staff stay in touch with equipment managers, like St. Louis's Buddy Bates, discussing plans for new uniform styles, supplying uniforms for players who have been traded from one team to another, and generally making sure that the quality and fit of each uniform is exactly what the team and players want.

The process for making new uniforms begins in the knitting room at Rawlings Plant #3 in Licking, Missouri.

There, high-speed knitting machines transform spools of polyester yarn into durable fabrics. On each machine, a loop of hole-punched paper opens and closes switches that operate the machine's automatic knitting needles. Different patterns of holes open and close the switches in different sequences, allowing Rawlings to knit fabric in different colors and patterns. While one machine, called a rib knitter, might be knitting orange, white, and blue trim material for uniforms for the Detroit Tigers, another, called a jersey knitter, knits yards of white fabric for shirts for the Los Angeles Dodgers. The knitting room clacks and pulses with mechanical noise. Fabric cascades off the jersey knitters at a rate of 9⅜ yards per hour. Workers move from machine to machine, changing pattern loops, replacing empty spools, inspecting the fabric for dropped stitches and other flaws. As with the inspection of gloves and baseballs, perfection is a byword.

Once a big batch of fabric has been knitted, it is run on rollers through a steaming vat of polyvinyl acetate. Students of adhesives will recognize polyvinyl acetate, or PVA, as the chief ingredient in Elmer's glue. Fabric used to make baseball uniforms is steeped in a watered-down bath of the stuff. The PVA prevents the edges of the fabric from curling and the fabric from slipping later when it is cut.

Meanwhile, patterns for different uniforms are produced in the pattern development and marker-making department, also known as the AM-5 Room, after the computer system that's used there. Computer technicians work with electronic styluses, drawing or modifying patterns, which appear in miniature on the computer screen. When a pattern is precisely to specification, the information is fed to an enormous high-speed plotter that prints the pattern to actual size on huge sheets of lightweight paper.

Bolts of treated cloth and cardboard copies of the patterns go to the cutting area. There, on long tables, workers layer the cloth in thicknesses up to eight inches, trace the patterns on the top layer, and, with high-speed electric knives, cut the cloth into a uniform's various parts. The first cut is very rough.

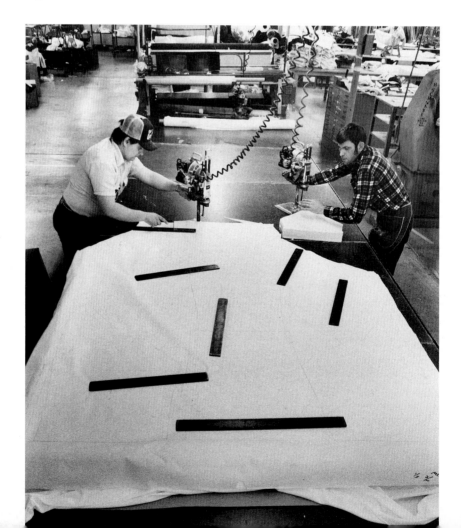

The final tracing and cutting are far more precise. The pattern is traced on the fabric with a fine-pointed pencil, and the fabric is cut with a razor-sharp circular knife.

Cut pieces are stacked, bundled, labeled, and sent to the sewing area. The buzz of the sixty-four sewing machines and the stacks of partially sewn uniforms give the area a distinct air of chaos. In fact, though, every seamstress knows her job, and every job is done well. While some seamstresses sew sleeves to shirt bodies, others sew belt loops to pants. Some sew buttonholes. Others sew on buttons. Some sew on letters, numerals, and trim. Others sew pockets, labels, and waistbands. On average, it takes about one and a half hours, from start to finish, to sew a uniform, and the finished result always looks handsome.

A whole separate section of the sewing area is devoted to turning out lettering and numerals. Using dies and stamping machines similar to those used for stamping out glove parts, workers in this department can create in cloth any numeral from 1 to 9, any name from ALLANSON to VALEN-ZUELA, any logo from ANGELS to EXPOS to RED SOX.

Another section of cutting and sewing can also perform any special modifications that players have requested in their uniforms. Some players, for instance, don't like hip pockets; they only want the seams faced where the pockets' openings would go. Other players specify sliding pads sewn into their pants' hips. Still others ask that the knees of their pants be widened to accommodate knee braces. And still others, like the owner of these pants, ask for hidden pockets to stash sunglasses, cigarettes, and gum.

A single, finished major league uniform — pants and shirt — costs $110 to $130. Teams order uniforms in sets of four per player — two for home and two for the road. As a player's uniforms are inspected and approved, tags are sewn beside the manufacturer's label, indicating the player's number, the year in which the uniforms were made, and the number of the set.

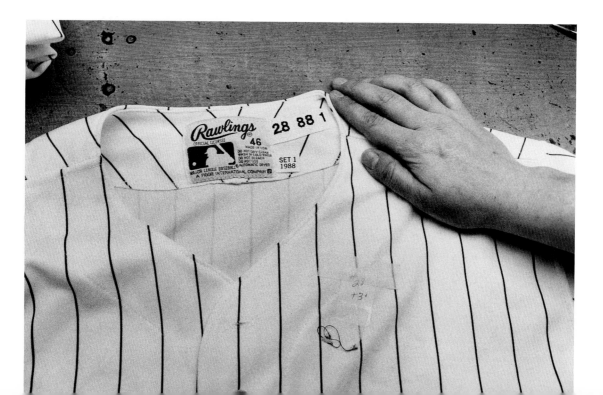

Then the uniforms are bagged and boxed and shipped to the teams that ordered them. If a player is traded to a new team, Rawlings can have his new uniforms, tailored precisely to his size, delivered to the team equipment manager within forty-eight hours from the time the order is received. It's an intense operation that's been in business for 101 years, and quality control is always critical. Still, there have been glitches. Not many years ago, the Cincinnati Reds brought up a hot rookie prospect in mid-season, and none of the extra shirts that the Reds' equipment manager kept on hand for such situations fit the newcomer. A frantic call was made to Rawlings. Could the Licking plant make a shirt fast? They could. They did. They made it faster, perhaps, than any shirt ever made in the company's history. The next evening, the eager rookie took to the field in the hastily sewn shirt. Before the first inning's end, sportswriters in the press box were smiling and nudging each other and guffawing. Some eager employee at Licking had failed to consult a map of Ohio. According to the lettering on the shirt, the rookie now played for "CINCINATI."

IV

Bat

From the bat rack in the visitor's dugout in Busch Stadium, the New York Mets' right-fielder, Darryl Strawberry, selects the bat he will use for tonight's game against the Cardinals. The bat he chooses is one of six in the rack with his name branded on it: D. STRAWBERRY. On the butt of the bat a code has been imprinted: 113A. That code identifies the model as his. When Strawberry talks about his bat, model 113A, he speaks of it in the manner of an artist discussing his brushes or a mechanic his personal set of tools. Wetting his lips, he says, "I like a bat that's long and tapered, with a thin handle so it feels relaxed in my hands. The grain at the end of the bat, the barrel, has to be tight. That's where the bat hits the ball. The bat I use is thirty-five inches long and weighs thirty-three ounces. With the handle so thin, most of the weight of the bat is in the barrel, where it should be, so I can get bat speed — momentum — to drive the ball. People think the thin handle means I crack a lot of bats, but I rarely do. I lose bats because people steal 'em." He laughs. Home runs have been sailing off this particular bat of late, and he radiates confidence holding it. "Yeah, no lacquer or varnish

or any of that stuff on my bats. Just bare wood and a little pine tar for the grip." His eyes turn toward the fences. "Excuse me," he says after a moment, "I've got to go do my stretching."

Model 113A is manufactured for Darryl Strawberry in Dolgeville, New York, by the Rawlings/Adirondack bat factory. Throughout the year, the company's log buyer, Pete Jaikin, travels a hundred-mile arc below the huge southern border of Adirondack State Park in search of northern white ash logs for baseball bats. He visits loggers at their job sites. "Got any ash for me today?" he asks. Sometimes they do, sometimes they don't. Northern white ash tends not to grow in large stands.

On this particular day in late spring, two loggers Pete visits, Ed Keeler and Jimmy Hulbert of Johnstown, New York, tell Pete they've found some ash in a hundred-acre forest they're selectively cutting just south of Little Falls. Pete says he'll buy any ash they take out. He accompanies Ed, who carries his chain saw, onto the tract. A half mile in, among younger maples and beeches, they find a number of mature northern white ash trees. "Stand back," Ed says. "Let's see how this looks."

On the third try, the saw starts. Its harsh whine shatters the green air. Ed makes a cut into the base of the tree, and pale chips fly onto the forest floor. He walks the Stihl saw around the tree's circumference, and, in a matter of seconds, the big tree groans on the holding wood. Ed cuts the saw's engine and backs away. Loud cracks and pops emanate from the tree's base. The tree wavers a bit. A moment later, with a rush of leaves and branches, it crashes to the forest floor.

Ed saws the tree below the first branches, and he and Pete have a look. It's a good tree, a "select," and yet would probably have become the victim of disease and insects if left standing. Pete feels he's saved the tree for a better fate. He knows it'll yield a lot of fine bats.

A few minutes later, Jimmy enters the forest driving a noisy, monstrous vehicle called a skidder, to which he chains the log and skids it back to the other logs at the landing. He pushes the logs — mostly maple, beech, and spruce, some cherry, a few ash — into a tidy pile and joins Pete and Ed at Pete's pickup truck. "Here's what we make out of ash," says Pete, showing Ed and Jimmy a sample bat he always carries with him. "Well, look at that," says Jimmy. "That's fine workmanship," says Ed. "The major-leaguers think so," Pete says.

In the late afternoon, a log truck rumbles onto the landing, and its driver, Dave Subik, loads the logs with the aid of a hydraulic grappler. The entire platform on which Dave sits can rotate, and, by operating six different levers, Dave can make the grappler pluck a log from the pile and lay it onto the truck bed as gently as if it were bone china.

When a load of northern white ash arrives at the Rawlings/
Adirondack sawmill in Dolgeville, a yard operator unloads it
with the aid of a grapple-skidder called a Pettibone Cary-Lift.

He stacks the logs in long rows and another worker scales the logs, that is, he determines their volume in board feet. A board foot is a unit of measurement equal to the volume of a board one inch thick and twelve inches square. The worker measures the diameter of the log, then consults a log-scale chart in the ledger he carries. The chart tells him exactly the number of board feet in a log eight to sixteen feet long and six to thirty inches in diameter. He finds the measurement, writes it on the butt of the log in black crayon, and he also writes it in the ledger. In this way, the mill knows exactly how much to pay a logger for his logs. Northern white ash logs fetch about four hundred dollars per thousand board feet. An ash log fourteen feet long and fourteen inches thick — an average dimension — contains 114 board feet of lumber and is worth $45.60.

The Pettibone Cary-Lift is on the move. Its hydraulically operated steel jaws drop a load of logs onto a link conveyer belt. A devilish grinding noise emanates from the low-roofed shed toward which the belt propels the logs. The debarker is working. A sure-handed worker sits inside a little booth operating levers that propel the debarker's spinning steel teeth over each log. Bark flies off the log like sparks. Wheels spin the log so that the debarker can remove every fragment of bark sheathing the log's wood. The manufacture of a bat for Darryl Strawberry has begun. It is a noisy beginning.

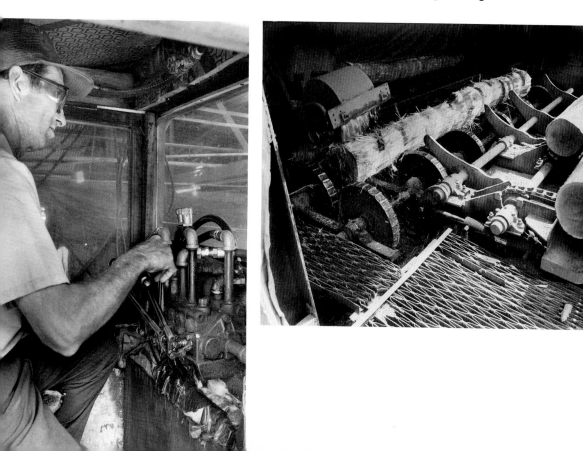

For the time being, it doesn't get any quieter. Once de-
barked, the pale, damp ash logs clatter along a conveyer to a
circular saw with a forty-eight-inch blade. So noisy is the saw
when it cuts, so shrill and high-pitched its whine, that every-
one who comes near it must wear earplugs. The blade cuts
the logs into forty-inch lengths as easily as a hot knife cutting
butter. Then a worker, manning a powerful hydraulic splitter
nicknamed Mr. T., splits the lengths into four-inch-thick
chunks.

One by one, each chunk is clamped at its ends into a different kind of cutting machine called a rough lathe. The rough lathe spins the chunk at high speed while a forty-inch row of blades noisily pares the chunk into a three-inch-round cylinder known as a billet. The blades do their work in six seconds. As billets are tossed on a table, it's difficult to remember that each was once an integrated fragment of a living tree.

Later, each billet is graded according to its quality. The best billets, graded "special," are destined to become pro-model baseball bats. Other billets, graded one, two, or three, are destined to become bats for the rest of us.

In pallets of three hundred, the billets are dried for three months in big warehouselike buildings called kilns. A system of gas furnaces heats each kiln to a temperature of 120 degrees, and fans draw the heated air over the billets. Since moisture tends to move to areas of lesser concentration, the moisture in the wood is drawn into the drier, heated air. Fans suck this air out of the building. Slowly, so that the wood doesn't crack, the billets are leeched of their moisture. After twelve weeks, only 6 percent of their moisture remains. Only then are the billets actually ready to be made into bats.

When the billets come out of the kiln, a forklift drives them a half mile down the road to the Rawlings/Adirondack bat factory. In the main cutting room, the billets are clamped one by one to a finish lathe, which cuts the billet into the rough shape of a bat.

Once the billets are cut on a band saw to thirty-seven-inch lengths, they're given over for weighing to Bill Steele, Rawlings/Adirondack's chief bat maker. A billet may weigh as little as forty-four ounces or as much as fifty-six, and the reason for the disparity is that even though the billets are all the same dimension, they're not all of the same density. "Some have more wood fibers and fewer open pores," says Bill, "so they weigh more."

On a rack in a mesh-enclosed space called the finish room, Bill stores the billets until it's time to make them into bats. But then it seems it's *always* time to do that. Orders like this one, from the New York Mets for twelve new bats for Darryl Strawberry, arrive at the factory daily.

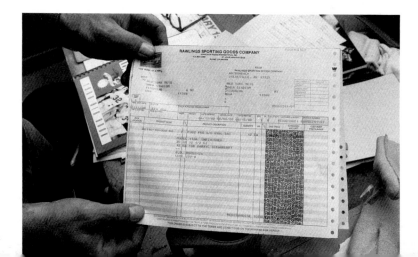

To make a bat for Darryl Strawberry, Bill starts by inserting the ends of a master model 113A bat into the uppermost pins, or chucks, of a machine called a copy lathe. He then goes to the billet bin, selects two fifty-one-ounce billets from the stock, and mounts these on the chucks below the master bat. The master bat is a little bit thicker, longer, and heavier than a finished model 113A, but it's perfect for Bill's purposes. And the copy lathe is an ingenious machine. As it

rotates the three lengths of wood, a measuring tool slowly runs along the surface of the master bat. The measuring tool is connected to two electric cutting blades below it. With the depth of their cuts controlled by the measuring tool, the blades move over the two billets, trimming them down to the dimensions of the master bat. In five minutes, Bill Steele has, in effect, *three* master bats. Two of them he will hand cut into finished model 113A's.

To guide him in his cutting of the bats, Bill fetches from the bat room a finished model 113A. The bat room is like a bat maker's library. In it, Bill can find a model of any Rawlings/Adirondack bat ever used by a major league player. Near Darryl Strawberry's 113A is a model 154A (Mike Schmidt), a DW20 (Dave Winfield), and a 113A (Gary Carter). Dale Murphy's 380B hangs beside Tony Gwinn's TG19. "It's kind of neat," says Bill, "seeing all these bats you've made and knowing who uses them."

Back in the finish room, Bill sets the bat room's model 113A on a metal stand behind his lathe, takes measurements from its different sections, and begins cutting the rough master to the same size. Wood chips fly when his knife touches the spinning wood. The knife sculpts the rough master: first the knob, then the handle, then the all-important barrel. With steady hands and a sharp knife, Bill sculpts a perfectly proportioned model 113A bat in less than ten minutes.

Sandpapering comes next — about a minute's worth, with eighty-grit sandpaper. Then Bill unchucks the bat, trims the excess wood off the knob with a band saw, and taps in the bat's model number with a set of heavy steel dies.

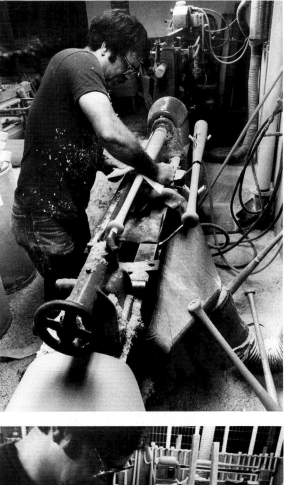

Except for its labels, the bat is finished. Bill Steele now takes it into the adjoining paint room where a silk-screening machine prints it in black ink with the Rawlings/Adirondack logo and an electric branding iron brands "***BIG STICK*** D. STRAWBERRY PROFESSIONAL MODEL" into its barrel. Bill knows that a bat stands a greater chance of cracking if a baseball strikes it against the bat's wide grain. For every player but one, he positions the labeling over that grain. Players then need only remember the old coaching adage, "Turn the label up" — that is, hold the bat so the label faces skyward when the bat is held over the plate — and they significantly reduce their risk of cracking the bat. For that one player who wants the label in a different place, St. Louis's catcher Tony Pena, Bill positions the labels over the narrow grain. Why? It's not that Pena enjoys cracking bats. He simply likes using the Rawlings/Adirondack logo and the words "***BIG STICK*** TONY PENA PROFESSIONAL MODEL" as a target for creaming baseballs.

Last step: the one-inch stripe, which can be a different color depending on the team. Bill mounts Darryl's bat on a system of rollers that spin it much as a lathe does. With a small brush and a can of enamel paint, he rings the bat in blue. Making bats as he does at a rate of seven dozen a day, Bill can fulfill orders from teams within ten days. When outstanding hitters meet him and learn he is the man who makes their bats, they typically shake his hand and thank him. "You send me good wood!" many exclaim. Once, in the visitor's dugout in Montreal, Bill met Dave Parker, the veteran outfielder, who was then playing for the Pittsburgh Pirates. Bill handed him his card and revealed himself as the maker of Parker's Rawlings bats. Parker smiled. "Well, I'll be using your bat tonight," he said. In his first at bat, Parker crushed the ball for a home run over the center-field fence. Parker went three for four that night. Bill Steele was quietly pleased. "I'll never forget that night. Parker thanked me for making him that bat, and then he got all those hits. The best was that home run. It soared over the fence. I'll never forget that."

V

Delivery

When Bill Smith arrives at Busch Stadium with Ozzie Smith's new glove, he finds Ozzie out near the batting cage with the Cardinals' left-fielder, Vince Coleman. Vince and Ozzie are talking about Vince's bat. At Vince's request, Bill Steele, at Rawlings/Adirondack, has scooped half an ounce of ash from the end of the barrel. On his lathe, Bill has tapered the handle of Vince's bat to the approximate shape of a cone. "Tommy Herr introduced me to this style bat," says Vince. "I'm a line-drive hitter and I like a bat with a big, long barrel so I can get good wood on any pitch. At the same time, I want the bat to feel comfortable in my hands — balanced — with the top not too heavy and the handle not too skinny. To balance the bat, and so I can get around on any pitcher in the league, I have Rawlings scoop, or cup, the end. That's a half ounce less bat I have to swing."

Ozzie says, "The only thing I feel about cupping a bat is that a ball hit off a cupped bat's end isn't going to travel as far as off a regular bat. But, it works for Vince. I like a more traditional bat. Every player has different preferences."

When Ozzie receives his new glove from Bill Smith, he goes into the Cardinals clubhouse and performs a minor alteration on it. He cuts a six-inch piece of soft adhesive called moleskin into a long oval and sticks it onto the back of the glove's first finger. A single season of games and practices can torture an infielder's catching hand. The index finger is the most vulnerable. Ozzie adds the moleskin to his glove to protect his index finger from bone bruises. "I like my glove a little stiff," he says, "with a relatively deep pocket. I spend a lot of time developing a glove's pocket in practice before I'll even think of using it in a game. A glove should feel like an extension of your hand. I use a small glove because an infielder doesn't need a big one. I soften the fingers of my glove with a lanolin-based leather conditioner, and I'm usually breaking in two gloves during practices for use later in games. How long does a glove last me? It depends. Here it is June, and I'm still using the same glove in games that I started spring training with. The weather has a lot to do with it. When the weather's hot, I sweat a lot. The glove starts to get waterlogged. When it gets too wet and heavy on my hand, I know it's time to call Smitty. Also, if I lose a glove, or it gets stolen, I always have one or two others broken in just in case."

From both the Cardinals' and Mets' clubhouses, more and more players come onto the field for practice. Darryl Strawberry appears with his Rawlings Pro TF-B, a slightly larger, slightly different version of the glove Ozzie Smith uses. "I've tried a lot of gloves," he says, "and I fell in love with this one. A glove has to feel comfortable, and this one does to me. I like its looseness, its flexibility, its deep pocket, the style of its web. I've had this glove since last year. If you take care of a glove, you can use it for three or four years, and once you get used to it, you don't want to give it up. Your glove is as important as your bat. If you're uncomfortable with it, you can be sure you're going to make errors."

Luis Alicea, one of the Cardinals' second basemen, likes a short-fingered glove "soft in the pocket, stiff in the fingers." He uses one glove a season, and during spring training he takes hundreds of throws and hundreds more ground balls to break it in. "I like the fingers open, not closed like a clamp or basket," he says, demonstrating how the glove's four fingers should be flared back for a ground ball. "If the glove is formed into a closed basket shape — look — only the first

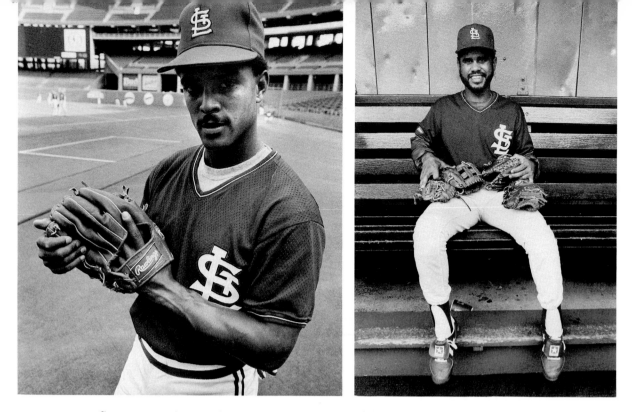

finger, web, and thumb can scoop the ball. But when it's formed into an open shape"— he flares its last three fingers — "the whole glove makes the catch."

Alicea's teammate, Jose Oquendo, has a special problem. Depending on his team's needs, on any given night he may find himself playing outfield, first base, second base, or third. Since each position requires a different glove, Jose has four: a Rawlings Pro DCT for first base, a Pro 2-HC for third base, a smaller Pro 15-X-TC for second base, and a Pro HC for the outfield. The biggest difficulty his versatility poses for him is adjusting his play from outfield to infield. "When I come in to play infield after playing the outfield," he says, "I run the risk of being lazy on ground balls. Using a big outfielder's glove can do that to you. As an infielder, I want to get down on the ball and stay down. I don't want to get lazy. I can't. So when I take infield practice, I use the smallest glove I have, my second baseman's glove, which forces me to stay down on ground balls. Then, even if I play third base that night and use my third baseman's glove, which is only a little smaller than my outfielder's, I know I'll stay down because I've practiced with a smaller glove. You see?"

When Bill Smith visits a ballpark, he uses it as an opportunity to meet with players using Rawlings equipment. Sometimes a player's uniforms need further fine-tuning, so Bill is available to listen to what the player wants, take measurements, and send the information back to the pattern makers, cutters, and seamstresses at Licking. In the Mets' clubhouse, Bill meets with first baseman Dave Magadan and Charlie Samuels, the Mets' equipment manager, in front of Magadan's locker.

"It's the pants," says Magadan. "The length is fine, but the waist is a little tight, and the legs are way tight around the thighs."

"We can fix," says Bill, taking measurements. "Charlie, where's the team go next after St. Louis?"

"Atlanta."

"We'll ship you four pairs there. Two days. Okay?" He apologizes to Magadan.

"Hey, that's okay," says Magadan. "Thanks a lot." He smiles and shakes Bill's hand.

Not all the baseballs that Rawlings ships to the major leagues end up being used in games. Many are autographed by players and used for charitable or promotional purposes. The fate of these baseballs that Charlie sets out for signing in the Mets' clubhouse? Souvenirs for Mets' fans, players' friends, and use as fund-raising tools for various charities.

The stadium's gates open. Spectators begin filling the seats. In the batting cage, a minor drama unfolds. Darryl Strawberry is taking batting practice, and now, after three or four sharp hits, he is starting to slam baseballs into the outfield seats. In his hands is the bat, model 113A, that Bill Steele made for him only weeks earlier. Baseballs manufactured in February shoot off this bat now, in June. Strawberry's form at the plate is unconventional. As the ball approaches, he lifts his right foot — for balance, he says —

cocking his right knee back, waggling the bat behind his left
ear. His right foot steps forward; his bat uncoils — *crack!* —
northern white ash meets pill, yarn, and cowhide. The ball
sails in a high parabola over the center-field fence, landing,
to a chorus of spectator gasps, among the seats. *Crack!* Strawberry hits another long ball. *Crack!* Another. Each travels in
the same high arc, and the flight of each ball seems, some-
how, unconnected to the slash of Strawberry's bat in the cage.

In the game that night, Ozzie Smith, wearing a baseball glove crafted for him by a dedicated group of people in southwestern Missouri, makes a number of brilliant catches. And Darryl Strawberry, using a bat turned to his specifications in a factory in upstate New York, hits his twentieth home run of the season. Viewing the game on television from his home in Dolgeville, Bill Steele feels a twinge of satisfaction. And Bill Smith, watching from a seat in the press box, smiles.

As Strawberry, in his perfect-fitting uniform, starts his victory lap around the bases, a kid, in the right-field seats, age twelve perhaps, catches the baseball that has sailed off Strawberry's bat. He stands, dazed and grinning, holding the ball aloft for all to see. He hands it to a man sitting next to him. The man stares into the ball as if it were crystal and, laughing, hands it back to the kid. They talk to each other animatedly. In the dugout, teammates are standing, high- and low-fiving Strawberry, who has made his triumphant return. The Mets' batboy has retrieved model 113A from home plate and now slips it back into the bat rack. In his place in the sea of red seats, the kid puts the ball in his pocket.

Acknowledgments

I am indebted to literally hundreds of people for their help during the writing and photographing of this book. I especially wish to thank Scott Smith, public relations manager at Rawlings, who arranged all my visits to the company's plants, drove me from St. Louis to Licking to Ava, tirelessly answered my questions about the company's manufacturing processes, and served as my liaison with the Cardinals and the Mets. Scott, *mirabile dictu*, is a transplanted New Englander, a fly-fisherman, and a Red Sox fan; more to the point, over the course of this project he became a friend.

Bill Smith, the manager for professional sales at Rawlings, and Ted Sizemore, Rawlings' vice president of baseball development, also answered a great number of my questions, both about the company and the major league clients it serves. My thanks to them both for their time, effort, and cooperation on behalf of this book.

Special thanks also goes to Paul Stickley, plant manager at the Rawlings plant in Licking; Roger Lueckenhoff and Randy Aden in quality control; Don Haught and Bob Clevenhagen in Ava; Bruce Mang, Bill Steele, and Pete Jaikin in Dolgeville; Dave Subik, Jimmy Hulbert, and Ed Keeler in Johnstown; and the wonderful Ruth Zayas in St. Louis.

Former Rawlings employee George Matchell demonstrates the baseball-stitching procedures that appear in these pages. Kate Peatman drew the cowhide diagram that appears in the opening chapter. The last two photographs in the book were taken by Richard Mackson for *Sports Illustrated*, and the picture of Ozzie Smith fielding a grounder appears courtesy of the St. Louis Cardinals. The three photographs of old-time baseball uniforms on page 45 appear courtesy of the National Baseball Library, Cooperstown, New York. For worse or better, all other photographs are mine.

Kip Ingle, public relations director for the St. Louis Cardinals, graciously allowed me to visit with various players at Busch Stadium, and Buddy Bates, the Cardinal's equipment manager, actually let me take pictures around the clubhouse. Thanks, too, to Frank Copenbarger, the team's assistant equipment manager, for teaching me, once and for all, how to mud up a big-league baseball, and to the press-box chefs at Busch Stadium for feeding me so far from home.

This book would not have been possible without the interest and cooperation of the players who appear in it. My great good thanks to Ozzie Smith, Vince Coleman, Tony Pena, Luis Alicea, Jose Oquendo, and Terry Pendleton of the Cardinals; and Darryl Strawberry, Dave Magadan, and Gary Carter of the Mets. Each of these players took time out of his busy pregame schedule to talk to me about his equipment preferences, and the care and thoughtfulness of their words impressed me deeply.

Jay Horowitz, public relations director for the Mets, and Charlie Samuels, the team's equipment manager, also deserve special thanks for giving me access to the Mets team and answering my questions about its equipment needs.

Warm thoughts and thanks to Karen Carpenter, Gita Mehta, Roe Marra, Tom Ettinger, and the world's greatest agent, Henry Dunow, in New York; John Keller, Betsy Groban, David Coen, and the rest of the children's-book staff at Little, Brown, in Boston; Tony and Sandy Urbaniak in Aberdeen, South Dakota; and former Los Angelinos Steve Geller and Karen Mankovich in Phoenix. As always, Pam, Andrew, and Sam were a thoughtful and supportive family; and the Johnson, Vermont, Minor League Team Two proved to be capable product testers of some of the equipment that appears in this book.

Finally, I wish to thank all the employees at Rawlings, past and present, who allowed me to speak with them and photograph them at work. Their interest in the project and their kindness and professionalism toward me were exemplary; they are living proof that, in at least one American company, excellence thrives.